A Thrill of Hope

Preparing Your Heart and Home for Him

Erin Gandy Stache

Copyright © 2019 Erin Gandy Stache

All rights reserved.

ISBN: 9781730710131

DEDICATION

I would like to dedicate this first published work to my husband, Jeremy, and our beautiful daughter, Bayley. I am thankful you are my people on this side of glory.

CONTENTS

	Introduction	1
1	A Thrill of Hope	3
2	All the Preparation	5
3	The First Evangelistic Message	7
4	Noah, the Flood, and a Rainbow	10
5	Father Abraham	12
6	We Will Go to Worship	15
7	I Will Not Let Go	18
8	O Come, All Ye Faithful	21
9	Judah and Tamar	23
10	Joseph and the Sovereign God	26
11	The Exodus, Moses and Jesus	28
12	Rahab	31
13	A Story of Great Provision	33
14	An Unlikely King	35

15	The Prophets	37
16	Silence	39
17	Joy to the World! The Lord is Come!	42
18	Zechariah: How Shall I Know?	44
19	Preparing the Way of the Lord	47
20	Mary, Did You Know?	50
21	All is Calm. All is Bright.	52
22	The Shepherds and All the Haste	54
23	The Gift of the Magi	56
24	Christ Was Born for This! Christ Was Born for This!	58
25	Christmas Day	61

Appendix

Preparing Your Home – Intentional Gatherings   63

Preparing Your Home - Recipes   65

A Thrill of Hope

INTRODUCTION

Our Thrill of Hope

Merry Christmas, friends!

I hope this Advent season finds you excited and anticipating the celebration of the birth of our Savior. There is so much to be thankful for this year, as we prepare to celebrate Christ's birth! However, I know the holiday season can be filled with mixed emotions as we approach Christmas Day. Some of you are grieving the loss of loved ones who will not gather around the table this year. There are others of you who are single and desire to spend this magical holiday with a spouse; I've been there. While others may be married and anticipating the arrival of their own child one day, yet the Lord has not opened their womb. You could be the overwhelmed mother of five who needs a break, or you might be the empty-nester who feels like her purpose has been lost without children at home. Wherever you find yourself this season, at this time, I'm glad you've decided to join in on this study.

As one who loves to sing Christmas carols, I could think of no better way to title this devotion than after a line from the 1847 hymn "O Holy Night."[1] Every time I sing this classic hymn, I am enamored by four seemingly insignificant words (in comparison with the rest of the song): "a thrill of hope". The words leave me breathless.

I like to imagine the writer of the hymn sitting in awe writing phrase after phrase. Generation after generation anxiously awaited their redemption and the fulfillment of the promise made to Adam and Eve in the garden. This hope manifested itself when Jesus came to earth. It is the center of the Christmas season. He was their thrill. He was their hope. He was their JOY! The same stands true for us!

---

[1] Adolphe Adam, "O Holy Night," 1847.

This Advent season may we be found like generations past who faithfully awaited the arrival of their King. Regardless of where you are in your current life situation, may we be found faithful and obedient as we await His Return!

I've got my pine scented candle lit, and I am ready to begin studying the stories of the men and women whose lives are a thread in the story of our redemption. Their stories, though mostly familiar, are woven throughout the course of history to show us one main objective - HOPE.

The official Advent season consists of the four Sundays leading up to Christmas Day. This study will begin on Sunday, December 1st and end on December 25th. The devotion for each Sunday of Advent will correspond to the candle traditionally lit on the Advent wreath; each candle represents something. Subsequent days will include some reading and writing/journaling (but no arithmetic!) Grab your Bible. Make this time special - location, hot coffee beverage, or a candle of the season. It's time to slow down and savor Him. The rest of your day, and the festivities will wait.

Note: Unless otherwise stated, all scripture references will be from the English Standard Version.

1
A Thrill of Hope

The First Candle of Advent: Hope

Scripture Reading: See below.

The moment Jesus entered the world over two thousand years ago, born of a virgin in a small stable, the weary world rejoiced! Everything changed. Those who had waited, desperate for the Messiah to arrive, were no longer searching. Their prayers were answered. Emmanuel. The world rejoiced because their hope had come!

This hope we have is not empty but is built on the promises of God. For those who lived before Christ's birth, their hope rested on what was to come. God continuously revealed Himself to His people and made covenant with them. These covenants and promises pointed to the Christ. We live on this side of His birth and the cross. Our hope rests on what God has accomplished through His Son and what will be when He returns!

On this first Sunday of Advent, let's search the scriptures to learn and understand the promises made and the faithful God who made them.

For each reference, read the passage. Write a description of the promise and to whom the promise was made. We will cover these more in the days to come.

Genesis 3:15

Genesis 9: 8-17

Genesis 12:1-3

Jeremiah 31:33-34

The hope we have does not have its origins in anything we could conjure up within ourselves. We have hope in our Savior, Jesus Christ, because God has revealed Himself to us and made us His people. Unlike the generations of Abraham, we no longer have to await the birth of the Messiah. Yet, we anxiously are left awaiting His return to take us home!

This holiday season let us face the day with renewed hope; hope that is not defined by wishful expectations but rather is defined by the work and love of Jesus Christ. Hope is a person, and His Name is Jesus.

<u>Journal:</u>

1) What are you excited about this holiday season?

2) How will the definition of hope from a Christian perspective change the way you view this holiday season?

2
All the Preparation

Scripture Reading: Matthew 1

Preparations come in all shapes and sizes, especially during the holiday season. Whether we are planning a party and a guest list; buying all the presents for everyone on our list; or decorating the house, preparations are necessary. But let's not forget one big part of the holidays - all of the baking of sweet treats and goodies that we allow ourselves to partake in just one time a year. The preparations for baking often require more than we think. We have to know what we are going to cook. We have to make the grocery list. We have to shop at said grocery store. We have to measure out the ingredients. One thing might have to be made before another component of the recipe can be finished. And on and on it can go. See what I mean? All the preparations lead to a final outcome - the taste of Christmas and all the memories that flood our minds when we take just one tiny nibble. Christmas cheer is found in food!

During the Christmas season, Christians observe Advent as a season of preparation for the celebration of the birth of Jesus. The word, advent, has its root in the Latin word adventus, which means coming. For years men and women anticipated the arrival of their Messiah. Some thought he would come as a ruling governor, while others assumed he would be a valiant warrior. Never would they expect Him to come as a babe and be born in a manger. The stories that lead up to the arrival of the Messiah reveal the anticipation and preparations these men and women made for years - They were looking to the day their King would arrive!

To be fair, their journeys were filled with disobedience, sin and rebellion; yet they looked to the day when He would come and knew it to be so.

We mark this holiday Advent season as a time of preparing our hearts for the celebration of Christ's birth. When the activities of Christmas crowd out our schedule, the dedicated time of studying the Word of God aligns our hearts and minds with the True meaning of Christmas, and we are able to prepare room in our hearts for this wonderful celebration.

Journal:

1) What preparations were made for Jesus' arrival? If you know anything of the prophecies of His birth, how were those fulfilled at His birth?

2) What would it require of you right now to prepare room in your heart and life for the celebration of Jesus' birth? This may require an intentional look at your calendar and commitments.

3
The First Evangelistic Message

Scripture Reading: Genesis 2 and 3

Out of all the animals created during those six days, there was still something missing. God formed man from the dust of the earth and "breathed into his nostrils the breath of life…" (Gen. 2:7). Man was created in the image of God - not exactly like Him, but with the ability to reason, speak and have relationships. When none of the animals were seen to be a helper suitable for a relationship with the man, God created woman from the man's rib. Adam and Eve were the first man and woman to be created and were given responsibilities and warnings regarding the garden in which they resided. The writer of Genesis, most likely Moses, records the Fall of man and his disobedience of God. Not only did the two believe God was withholding something "good" from them, but they also believed their ways were better than His. By eating from the Tree of the Knowledge of Good and Evil, Adam and Eve disobeyed God and exalted themselves above His instructions. It wasn't until recently that I discovered the pair's desire to make their plans more prominent than God's. They somehow believed they had a better understanding of their surroundings than God did, and so they ate.

As a result, God cursed the deceitful serpent, the woman and the man. The snake would be limited to its belly. There would be pains in labor for the woman. There would be a "hard row to hoe", quite literally, for the man. It always seems quite dismal (as it should) for the man and woman, until something marvelous happens. In the midst of all that seems to be falling apart for the man and woman, we see a snippet or two of hope.

The Lord God does not forget the people He has created. He proclaimed a promise after issuing the curses: "I will put enmity between you and the woman, and between your offspring and her offspring: he shall bruise your [the serpent's] head, and you shall bruise his heel" (Gen. 3:15). In all of scripture these verses are referred to as the protoevangelium, or the first gospel. This is the first ray of hope given to fallen humanity. It's the first and THE best ray of hope for me and you!

I can almost hear the sighs of relief from Adam and Eve. Can you imagine knowing you have just royally messed up and your God proclaims that He will ultimately have victory, giving hope in such a despairing situation. The Seed of woman will rise above the serpent's attempts and will secure victory - a marvelous victory - for humanity! God had not forgotten His people and gave a thrill of hope to the man and woman standing before Him - guilty of sin, dependent on grace.

Though Adam and Eve were banished from the garden, the Lord did not allow them to leave until there was a covering over their bodies. God provided them with animal skins to cover their nakedness. I love the protoevangelium for everything it means, but this act rocks me to the core! From the moment sin was present, a blood sacrifice was being made to cover sin. An animal's life was sacrificed to cover their nakedness, their shame. This act sheds light on the future sacrificial system for the Israelites established by the law and ultimately the shedding of blood through Christ that secures our redemption. To tie these two aspects together: the seed of the woman, Jesus Christ, sacrificed His own life to cover our shame and nakedness. In Him, we are forgiven and made righteous. Is that not just the most wonderful thing you've heard? Not only will there be final victory for humanity, but there will also be a covering to cover all the shame and sin, so that we might walk freely!

I've referred to this scenario quite a few times over the last few years, but I just imagine Adam and Eve trying to piece those leaves together to present themselves to God when He was calling out to them in the garden. Leaves are flimsy and probably did not suffice for the cause. Yet, God stepped in and gave them an even greater covering. How many times do I try to cover it all up - make my mistake not so big. And here He is offering the greatest robe we could ever where given by His Son. "The weary world rejoices."

Journal:

1) When we find ourselves like Adam and Eve attempting to cover ourselves with our own version of fig leaves, how does the Truth of the protoevangelium/Genesis 3:15 give us hope that our own feeble attempts are not necessary?

2) Read Revelation 19:6-8. What is difference between the coverings mentioned here and those for Adam and Eve? What are the similarities? Who gives them? What does it cost? etc.

4
Noah, the Flood, and a Rainbow

Scripture Reading: Genesis 8:13- 9:17

I find the story of Noah and the flood to be an interesting one. We know the Lord's anger burned against the corrupt generations that walked the earth at this time. In our finite minds we don't fully grasp God's anger and see it as somehow unholy for the One, True God to have anger of this capacity. And yet, His anger is a righteous anger; it is justified. In *Knowing God*, J.I. Packer explains His anger to be justified because of the worship a holy God deserves and demands[2]. Like a husband would be jealous of his wife's attention elsewhere, so our God longs for us with a holy anger and love. The two are conveniently paired together. He demands total obedience to Himself and has the power to do whatsoever to those who do not revere His Name.

In the middle of the corrupt peoples is found a man by the name of Noah. Our childhood memories and felt boards recollect his building of the ark and the animals going inside two by two. I recently read the ark referred to as a "floating zoo." We know his family was with him and plenty of food was stored for the rains that would come for 40 days and 40 nights. Yet, there is more to the story of Noah than our five year old Sunday School minds should hold onto.

Noah and his family were spared the floods. They found favor with God. It was not any act or work that secured Noah's salvation from the floods, but it was God's grace and faithfulness. You see, God made a promise to man and woman in the garden. He would send a Seed who would crush the head of the serpent. This promise had to be fulfilled. Generations must continue until the Messiah came. God's faithfulness to Himself thus rendered Noah protected. Noah's

---

[2] J.I. Packer, "Knowing God," (Downers Grove, IL: InterVarsity Press, 1973).

family was the remnant that would lead to the mighty fulfillment of the garden promise.

The story of Noah signifies God's faithfulness to me/for me like never before. In short, He does not go back on His Word. He is faithful to His cause. He does not change His mind like the shifting waves of the sea. God knew humanity needed redemption. Instead of completely wiping out the human race, which would have been completely justified because He is God, the Lord saved a family for His redemptive purposes.

When the waters receded, God made covenant with Noah. Noah emerged from the ark and built an altar to worship God. It is there God made the promise to Noah and his family to "never again curse the ground because of man" (Gen. 8:21). A rainbow is placed in the sky as a symbol of that covenant. During seminary, my professor told us this rainbow symbolized a bow, as in a bow and arrow used for hunting. Because it was placed in the sky and turned away from the earth, it meant God would never wipe out humanity again. It should be noted theologians vary on their opinions of this meaning. Though we may never know with exact certainty I do love the visual picture of the rainbow representing an actual bow. Our creative God only allows the rainbow to appear in the sky after the presence of water. How timely and wonderful for us! The rains and the rainbow remind us of God's love and His purpose!

Journal:

1) How does the Lord's blessing to Noah in Genesis 9 coincide with Genesis 3:15?

2) How does Genesis 6:5 explain the sin nature of man and its presence from birth?

3) Read Genesis 11. How does the story of the Tower of Babel relate to the people of Noah's day prior to the flood?

5
Father Abraham

Scripture Reading: Genesis 12, 15

If you grew up in a church home, then chances are you sang "Father Abraham." We know the next few lines proclaim Abraham had many sons. But this was not so from the beginning. Though we can readily hum this church song from our youth, the deeper meaning behind the words represent a promised fulfilled and a people of God.

Abraham formerly known as Abram was called by God to leave his familial territory and take his wife and nephew to a place God would show them — the land of Canaan. Without doubts and fears, Abraham packed his belongings and moved forward on a promise given Him by a God he had yet to fully know. That's right. Abraham and his wife, Sarah, were pagan worshippers. They did not know God or obey Him at the time God chose them. If this passage offers you nothing else, hear this: God chose them not because of anything they did to acquire or provoke His affections.

In the middle of God's command to leave the homeland, He issued yet one more shocker that probably raised a few eyebrows: "And I will make you into a great nation" (Gen. 12:2). We need to pause for a moment. God promised this to a man who had never faithfully worshipped Him before. He promised this to a man who was old. He promised this to a man who only had a nephew and thus no children of his own. God promised Abraham he would have as many children as stars in the sky and grains of sand on the shore.

If you're like me, I tend to look at my circumstances and just think "No God, you can't do that in this situation." Abraham did something similar. He had resigned himself to the fact that his nephew, Lot, would be his heir and all the promises of God would be fulfilled through him. Not so. God promised a child to Abraham, his own flesh and blood by his wife Sarah. In that moment, Abraham believed God and it was credited to him as righteousness.

We know the story takes some twists and turns of its own; there are emotional highs and emotional lows. There are some just plain bad decisions made. There is impatience and unbelief on several levels. But in the end, Abraham's heir comes from Sarah's closed womb and is named Isaac. I love how Paul phrases Abraham's belief in his letter to the Romans:

> In hope he believed against hope, that he should become the father of many nations, as he had been told, "So shall your offspring be." He did not weaken in faith when he considered his own body, which was as good as dead (since he was about a hundred years old), or when he considered the barrenness[a] of Sarah's womb. No unbelief made him waver concerning the promise of God, but he grew strong in his faith as he gave glory to God, fully convinced that God was able to do what he had promised. That is why his faith was "counted to him as righteousness. (Rom. 4:18-22).

Abraham hoped against hope. That's it. When the situation seemed pretty dismal and like nothing was going to come to fruition, Abraham still held out hope. When he looked at his wife who was well beyond the child-bearing age, he still held hope. And why?

Abraham held hope because he believed in the God who had changed his life, his course, who had called him from his homeland. He believed this God would do exactly what He said he would do, even though he [Abraham] couldn't fully grasp it. He believed HIM.

This holiday season could bring in a lot of uncertainties in your life, as we enter a new year. I don't know where you are and what is going on in each of your circumstances. What I do know is that life isn't always perfect. It's not always the image we put on social media, and we all have our "junk". But like Abraham, we can hope against all hope that this isn't all there is and that we anxiously await the return of our Savior who will take us home. Doesn't that sound foreign sometimes? It does for me, but the Truth of that is so much greater than my good or bad days. We hope against all hope that He will return. He has told us He will. And now we wait — walking in faithfulness and obediently.

Journal:

1) How was Abraham's call to leave his homeland a step of faith for him and his family? What would have been the implications if Abraham had not believed God and decided to stay right where he was, rather than move forward?

2) What in your life is pushing you to have "hope against hope" and believe in the goodness and sovereignty of God this holiday season?

6
We Will Go to Worship

Scripture Reading: Genesis 22

Are you ready for this? The story of Abraham and Isaac on the mountain is quite possibly one of my most favorite stories from history because it serves as a precursor to the sacrifice of Christ on the cross! The two go hand in hand; it wasn't until I fully understood this aspect of Genesis 22 that I savored this story for its richness. The unyielding faith of Abraham; the sacrifice as worship; and, the substitution provided in the thicket leave me in awe of the Worthy God we serve.

As a quick recap of what you've read, God has instructed Abraham (name has changed at this point) to take his only son, Isaac, and sacrifice him as a burnt offering on the mountain. Abraham gathers the wood and supplies leading his son and servants to the dedicated spot. However, only Abraham and Isaac will go to the place of sacrifice. The patriarch looks to his servants and says, "I and the boy will go over there and worship and come again to you" (Gen. 22:5). Let's pause for a moment of effect. Here is Abraham. He has heard from God's mouth the promise to provide him an heir, to make him a great nation, and he sees this promised son standing in front of him. Yet, in great faith Abraham moves forward to sacrifice his son as a form of worship. He believed God could and would fulfill his promises, despite the obedient sacrifice he was making of Isaac. And to make it even more impactful of a moment— he called it worship!

Before moving on, I want to briefly focus on worship here. At Christmas time, there are many beautiful hymns and Christmas concerts that fully engage our hearts to worship the newborn King. Yet, worship is in other forms. Worship is in the hard! How often do we fail to see worship in the sacrifice. Whether it be the giving of our time, our money, our attention, it can all be worship to the glory of God in the right capacity. The mom, who is wiping up the spilled milk for the third time that day, can worship God in the moment.

The single girl, who who desires a Christmas date under the mistletoe, can worship God through the desire by sacrificing and giving it Him. The grieving widow can sacrifice her own mourning to mourn with others. Worship can be done in the hard! We don't really want to call it worship, nor do we even feel like it. But Abraham, with eyes focused on the Lord, went to worship. And now back to the rest of the story.

Though Isaac questioned his father as to where the animal for sacrifice would come from, Abraham confidently replied: "God will provide for himself the lamb for a burn offering, my son" (Gen. 22:8). God would provide. He would provide what they needed in that moment. Yet, Abraham faithfully strapped his only son to wood they had hauled painstakingly up the mountain. He readied the fire. He drew his knife-gripping hand in the air ready to bring it down on Isaac, and the Lord intervened. The gracious of our God. The faithfulness of Abraham. The obedience. It's too much to grasp. And then there's more. In the thicket next to their set up was a ram caught by the thorns. The ram would be the sacrifice instead of Isaac.

What a beautiful picture we gain here of the practice of substitutionary atonement! One would die in the place of another. This picture extends itself more clearly in the greatest act of substitutionary atonement we will ever know - Christ's life for our life. The great sacrifice of his own life, though not caught in the thicket but still wearing a crown of thorns, appeased the wrath of God; it set us free from the penalty of sin and death; and, it united us with our Father. Because of Christ being our substitute, "the weary world rejoices." Do you see why this story grips me as a child of God? We need not separate the Old Testament from the New and believe they don't relate. No, Christ is in all from beginning to end - Genesis to Revelation.

Journal:

1) What is something in your life that is material for sacrifice now that will free you to worship the Lord?

2) Read Matthew 19:16-26 - The Story of the Rich Young Ruler. Compare the young man's heart for worship to that of Abraham's.

7
I Will Not Let Go

Scripture Reading: Genesis 32

Scripture consistently refers to God in the Old Testament as the God of Abraham, Isaac and Jacob; they were the patriarchs - the chosen men through which the promises of God would be fulfilled. Remember God had promised Noah He would never destroy humanity again, and then came Abraham to which He promised to bless the nations, the world through his family. Jacob is the grandson of Abraham. Through some trickery and deception, Jacob manages to gain the family birthright and receives his father's blessing - at the great expense of angering his brother, Esau and having his life put on the line. In the words of someone great I'm sure, I could only look at Jacob and say, "RUN!"

Though all of Jacob's life events up until this point took place under the umbrella of God's sovereignty, it is important to note that Jacob has found himself in a less than favorable position. After acquiring two wives, Rachel and Leah, from his uncle Laban, Jacob prepared to return to his homeland and to see his brother again. A wise one, that Jacob, he prepares gifts to send ahead of him to Esau as a way of easing into the situation after years of hurt. Before their meeting, Jacob separates from his family and spent the night in the desert.

This wrestling. This struggle. This bout during the night, that left Jacob with an out of place hip socket, can best be described as Jacob being broken before the Lord. Jacob wrestled with God that night and was humbled before his Lord. Up until this point Jacob had been crafty in many of his ways. He had deceived his brother. He tricked his father. He was on the run from his brother. He experienced strife with Laban. And yet, this was the very man God had sovereignly chosen to lead His people and promised to bless the nations through him.

Jacob wasn't perfect and hadn't done anything to gain the merit of God. God's wrestling with him in the desert humbled him before the One who would lead him in the days to come. Jacob cried aloud in the battle, "I will not let you go unless you bless me" (Gen. 32:28). Can you hear it? Can you hear the dependence on the Lord? To me it sounds like this, "I'm not giving up. I'm not letting you go until you bless me because I need you. I need you to move forward and I can't do it on my own." I can almost hear the pants of desperation in Jacob's voice. Though God had spoken to him in dreams and showed him visions, Jacob had kind of acted on his own accord until now. And here we find him completely broken before the Lord and dependent on Him for His blessing.

I will fail miserably to put into words all this passage of scripture means to my life. It is one of those passages that have encouraged me tremendously during days of doubts and unbelief. The wrestling with God is difficult when we are in those tough seasons. Just like Jacob, we can find ourselves "doing life" on our own terms and just riding the waves of our own desires. When the hard times enter in, we find ourselves in a pit, and the wrestling begins. But isn't it grace that God even allows us to wrestle with Him? It is during those bouts that we find ourselves humbled in His presence and submitting to Him in a way we never have before. I truly believe Jacob would not have been able to efficiently lead the people of God with the attitude he had before his night alone with God. I also believe we are unable to do the thing(s) God has called us to until we are humbled by Him and refuse to let go until we receive the blessing.

Be encouraged friend. Whatever it is you are experiencing this Christmas season pales in comparison to the knowledge of our Savior coming to be the propitiation for our sins. We might wrestle and fight, but our God is using each of those moments to show us our need for Him and for the Savior. In Him, "our soul has found it's worth."

Journal:

1) Have you ever wrestled with God and emerged humbled before Him?

2) How does God use our fears and worries to turn our hearts to trusting Him?

8
O Come, All Ye Faithful

Second Candle of Advent: Faith

Scripture Reading: Hebrews 11

"O Come, all ye faithful — joyful and triumphant!"[3]

The second candle of the Advent wreath represents faith. The difference between hope and faith can be a bit muddy, so I'm going to do my best to distinguish the two for us. Hope is a confident trust, while faith is a commitment to follow based on the hope one has. Does that make sense? Because of the hope we have in Christ, our commitment to follow and believe God is manifests itself through our faith. Hope and faith are thus easily intertwined.

Write Hebrews 11:1 below.

Now write down the names of several individuals found in this "roll-call" of faith. Describe how they walked in faith.

At the center of our faith is Jesus Christ. Paul wrote to the Corinthians in his first letter, "And if Christ has not been raised, your faith is futile and you are still in your sins" (1 Cor. 15:17). I remind myself of Christ's birth often, especially when I get hung up on

---

[3] John Francis Wade, "O Come, All Ye Faithful," 1744.

something I've done and my works. Our faith would be worthless if it weren't for Jesus. This verse puts my faith into perspective. My faith is not about me but is about Him. Without Christ's birth, death, and resurrection, our sin would not have been atoned for, and we would not be redeemed. We would still stand guilty before the Holy God.

We have to celebrate Christmas with Easter in sight. It makes all the difference. Christmas is not just about a baby being born, though this story be all too familiar. It is more importantly God's redemptive plan coming to fruition — God gets the glory for every part of it.

Our faith begins with the promises of God, is set in motion at the birth of Christ, is solidified in His resurrection, and will be finalized at His return!

Journal:

1) Why is Christ the center of the Christian faith? Why was His birth, death, and resurrection necessary?

9
Judah and Tamar

Scripture Reading: Genesis 38, Genesis 49: 8-12, Matthew 1:3

I've always found the story of Judah and Tamar to be one of those "Pardon the Interruption" stories. It's like the friend of the group who decides to tell a completely random and off-topic story rather than go with the flow of normal conversation. (Hello, I'm that friend.) To be fair, I had never really done any research into the purpose of their story and just left it at "it must be important because Moses included it in Genesis." That was enough for me at the time but not anymore.

Without getting into too many specifics regarding Judah and Tamar, we must note the encounter the two had. There was deception. She was essentially portrayed as a prostitute. He grieved the loss of his wife by employing a prostitute. There was more deception. I see a trend. This is the story for the soap operas! With all these moments to make a girl blush, we can see why it's easy to wonder why this was included in scripture.

But before we dismiss it altogether, let's look at Tamar. Tamar was the wife of Judah's firstborn son, Er. He did not obey God and married outside of the Israelite community by taking Tamar as a wife — just as his father had done. Though we do not know for certain, it is generally assumed Tamar was a Canaanite woman. Er was so wicked in the sight of the Lord that God put him to death. Tamar was left without a husband or children to carry on the family name. The legacy and importance of children during this time in history was crucial. Children defined heritage, purpose and a sense of being. In this way, it may be easy for some of us to identify with Tamar.

And yet despite her nationality, deception and what would seem to us as an inappropriate relationship, the Lord redeemed this woman and her situation by blessing her with twin boys — Perez and Tamar. Again, this story could go unnoticed and we chalk it up to more descendants for the tribe of Jacob, but there is more to it. In Genesis 49, Jacob gives blessings to each of his sons, and though Joseph had always been the favored child, here we see a turn of events. Judah is given the blessing of having a familial line that will rule and hold the scepter for Judah. The birth of Perez, by Tamar, will play a role in the eventual rise of King David to power and our forever King, Jesus. I love what the ESV Study Bible says about this blessing:

> "This sets the tone for the chief aspect of messianic expectation in the OT: the way that Abraham's blessing will come to the Gentiles will be by the ultimate heir of David reigning and incorporating the Gentiles into his benevolent empire."[4]

Tamar is a Gentile herself and not originally of the Jewish people. Her incorporation into the ancestral line that will bring the blessing to the nations is not to go unnoticed! Tamar's pivotal role is noted again in the book of Ruth and Matthew's Gospel.

On this morning of Advent, I want to remind you (and myself) that in some way we are all Tamar's. We all have our failure moments that we deem to ourselves unworthy of kingdom involvement. Often I have this sense of being a failure as a wife and mom. I sometimes think I could be more friendly to others, more compassionate — more everything. And the result of all of that is feeling as if I'm just not enough. This year while studying Jacob and his sons, the Lord showed me the importance of Tamar in the story of our redemption. Unlikely to us but not to Him. We assume that the person who has it all together with matching Christmas outfits and a home decorated to the nines is the woman who is being used by God for the multitudes. And yes, she certainly could be, but she also has her moments too. She is also a sinner, if you want me to put it really bluntly. Tamar, you and I are all sinners standing before a holy God. We have all sinned against our holy God and are in need of his grace for salvation. Those of us who are believers gratefully rely on Christ's righteousness for our salvation — and not our pasts, present or future.

---

[4] "Genesis 49: 8-12," The ESV Study Bible (Wheaton, IL: Crossway, 2013), 134.

Dear friends, I wish I could say that I do this well. If I did I would be self-righteous. My husband reminds me quite often of our sanctification and the daily refining that must take place in our lives as believers. Tamar is not excluded from this. May we rejoice in a good Father who redeems us and restores us and uses us for His glory! When we fail, He has something already planned for that moment to be used to bring honor and glory to His Name, might it be our own humility turned to praise His sufficiency?

This Christmas let us not boast in our failures or our successes, but let us boast in Him alone!

Journal:

1) Do you allow your past or present to hinder you from believing you are accepted and loved by God? Do you feel unlikely?

2) How has God used some moment of failing in your life to bring glory to His Name?

10
Joseph

Scripture Reading: Genesis 42 and 45

It may seem odd for us to be studying Joseph in the midst of Jesus' familial line, yet it is with great intent that we look into the life of this patriarch.

There is much to say about Joseph's life. There was a colored coat that landed him sold into slavery because his brothers were jealous. He helped Potiphar in Egypt but was eventually thrown into prison on false accusations. He interpreted dreams for some pretty important people including Pharaoh. And he eventually landed in a prominent position in Egypt storing rations for the famine to come. All of this is important because of what we read in Genesis 42.

Joseph's family — including Jacob and the line of Judah through which the promised Seed would come — were affected by the famine. They are in need of food and find themselves in Egypt before Joseph asking for grain. And yet, they don't know it is their brother at the moment. We've already read the details of this encounter in our scripture reading for today, so I want to highlight this: God knew. God was in control. God never left His people.

Wow.

A man like Joseph could have easily been put in many other circumstances. He could have still been in prison. He could have died at any point along the way. He could have been bitter or angry or shown a lack of compassion to his brothers. But that wasn't the case. Read Genesis 45:5-8 again.

While there isn't a significant connection between Joseph's descendants and Jesus, it is God's hand through the life of Joseph that preserved the line of Judah. Joseph's position in Egypt, despite all the circumstances up until this point, allowed for the remnant of

Israel to be sustained. This remnant was kept and restored and protected — as we will see tomorrow it also flourished dramatically.

I'm reminded the holiday season can be one of the most joyous times of the year, while it can also be one of the most difficult. Our expectations meet our reality, and we can easily sink into a pit of frustration or despair. Looking at the life of Joseph, I'm certain the expectations of his life were never to be in a muddy, dank prison cell.

But God. God is greater than our expectations. We can be assured of that. Just like Joseph's family, He is always at work to preserve us and keep us for His work. Though we may not understand it today, He is working!

Journal:

1) What are your expectations for this Christmas season? Are they unruly? Are they focused on the right things?

2) How has God's hand been displayed in your life? I promise it's His hand and not your own. By recapping His hand and guidance, we can better see His faithfulness.

11
The Exodus, Moses and Jesus

Scripture Reading: See below.

Up until this point, we have studied the richness and foundation of a familial line who have allowed us to catch glimpses of God's promises being fulfilled. Though we do not have the full picture just yet, scripture continuously points to the Messiah, Jesus Christ.

Before we begin today's study, which will be more interactive and require more, we need a little background since we are skipping a few of the details in between.

The book of Genesis ends with 77 people in Jacob's family who have settled in Egypt due to the famine. This is far from the multitudes God initially promised Abraham. However, many pharaohs later we see the Hebrews have increased in numbers by leaps and bounds. The population is of such increase they have begun to intimidate the Egyptian rulers, and the pharaoh enforces harsh labor conditions. God calls Moses, a man from the tribe of Levi, of be the one to lead His people out of Egypt. The task wasn't easy — Moses felt ill equipped; the plagues didn't change the heart of the pharaoh; and, the Hebrews were quite skeptical. Though they saw Red Sea part and walked on dry ground, they still grumbled and complained wanting to eat the scraps of Egypt rather than the fruits of the Promised Land. They continued to be rebellious and hard-hearted despite all God had done.

I wanted to take today's time for us to explore some of the correlations between the Israelites' exodus and Moses and the glimpses of Jesus Christ that were very apparent. yet somehow missed. Like the Hebrews, our eyes are often focused on the bigger concepts of this story that we fail to see how Christ is woven into this story (Yes! Even here!). The people had been promised "one who would crush the heel of the serpent" (Gen. 3:15), but because of their grumblings they had missed the promises of Christ in the midst of it all.

Read each of the scripture pairs - one from the Old Testament and one from the New Testament. Write in your journal how each relate to one another. Remember these events happened many, many years apart from one another, and yet the same God reveals Himself to His people.

Jesus as the Passover Lamb - Exodus 12 and 1 Corinthians 5:7

The Bronze Serpent - Numbers 21:4-9 and John 3:14-18

Jesus as Manna from Heaven - Exodus 16 and John 6:35

Jesus as Living Water - Exodus 17:1-7 and John 4:4-26

These people, the Israelites, had just a sampling of the Savior to come, and they missed it. They missed His grace in passing over their homes with doorposts covered in blood. They missed being saved by looking to the bronze serpent. They missed the provision of the manna from heaven. And, they missed the water that poured forth from the Rock, who was Christ. I am often astounded and amazed at the connections we've made today with each of these scripture pairs. God was showing the people a peek into what it would be like when the Promised One would come; all of the experiences after crossing the Red Sea point to Christ. Their temporary, physical needs would be of no concern anymore, but their eternal, spiritual needs would be met. He is the final answer to our greatest needs.

In our own sin, we don't need just another "quick fix". My mind often wanders to some sort of self-help of the Bible. The help we need, which is highlighted from Genesis to Revelation, is Jesus. Paul says, "For there is no other name given under heaven by which men might be saved" (Acts 4:12).

Journal:

1) Do you miss Christ in *Christ*mas? Just like the Israelites witnessed God's hand time and again, they still managed to complain and not see what God was doing for them. What are some practical ways you and your family can put Christ first this holiday season? PS- There are still plenty of days to do a U-turn!

12
Rahab

Scripture Reading: Joshua 2 and Joshua 6

Rahab is one of three women in the genealogy of Jesus who was not of Jewish descent. I find this amazing and impactful because of what it means for the Gentile, such as myself! We are welcomed into the covenant community of faith as God's children. He made that very clear thousands upon thousands of years ago by calling men and women outside of the Israelite nation to follow him.

In preparing our hearts for this Christmas season. I want to note several things about the story of Rahab that impacts our lives, even now — especially now.

First, God valued women. Never is there a question of a female's worth in God's eyes. From the beginning, God made Eve a helper, a helpmate, for Adam. This was not meant as a degrading term but an honorable position. Because of the fall of man, our thoughts want to twist what God originally deemed as good for the roles of man and woman. If sin had never entered the world, we would never be prone to question if God truly loves women. BUT HE DOES! God chose Rahab, a prostitute living in Jericho, to protect the Israelite spies. God chose Rahab, a woman, out of all the people in Jericho to house these men in her home. God chose Rahab as the one who would be saved because of her faith when Jericho was conquered. She hung the scarlet thread outside of her window as promised. But, let it be clear, she displayed the scarlet thread because she had heard of what God had done, and she believed He loved her! Rahab responded in faith.

Second, God's grace is greater than our sin. When the Israelites returned to capture the city, the spies remembered Rahab's faithful assistance and went to save her. Rahab was known to be a prostitute in the city of Jericho. And yet, because of her faith, she was saved. She was saved *despite her sin*. God's grace is not based on what we have done or haven't done in our past. He does not extend grace based on our works or how we measure up. And yet, thought we would claim to agree with this statement, many of us sit in shame over a sin of our past, or we work so hard to prove ourselves to Him that we are barely making it. Though Joshua physically rescued Rahab, God gave her eternal salvation. She became a part of Abraham's family and would be used in a mighty way.

Read Matthew 1:5. Rahab is _____'s mother.

Our culture sends us so many mixed messages about our worth and value; all of which are wrong. Today, and every day, know that you are loved by a mighty God who fights for us and cares for you! He has met your GREATEST need through Christ, which is why we celebrate Christmas and Easter. Let us not forget this truth!

Journal:

1) Has the culture caused you to question how God loves and uses women?

2) Is there anything in your past or present that is causing you to believe you are outside of God's forgiveness and grace? (Note: This is NOT the case.)

3) Where does our soul find its greatest worth? Note the story of Rahab here.

13
A Story of Great Provision

Scripture reading: Ruth 1-4

The book of Ruth is nestled in the Writings portion of the Old Testament and is found to be one of the books of the Bible where there is little to no mention of God; and yet, His sovereign hand can easily be seen throughout the course of Ruth's life. The part of Ruth's story that we easily remember is the fact that she left her homeland and committed her life to take care of her bitter mother-in-law, Naomi. While no one desires to have a bitter mother-in-law, Ruth saw it as her duty to take care of this woman and provide for her. Despite having lost her husband and being without children, she put aside any expectations of her own life to take care of another. Yet, there is another layer to Ruth's life that can't go unnoticed. It is the very aspect of her story that ushers her into the family line of Jesus.

Before we begin, where was Naomi's family living originally before heading to Moab? (Ruth 1:1)

Bethlehem! This is where Jesus would be born years later! I find it to be quite amazing Elimelech took his family away from Bethlehem — where God's people were dwelling — and to the foreign land of Moab, which was Israel's enemy. Though Elimelech's sons married foreign women, God guided the remaining family members back to Bethlehem. He provided grain for a Moabite woman in the fields of a man named Boaz. Boaz's kindness to Naomi and Ruth ultimately are display of God's kindness and graciousness to us.

With that being said, we will now turn our attention to second layer of Ruth's story. Ruth was a foreign woman who remained faithful to Naomi and in so doing became a follower of God. She believed God and yet was not an Israelite by nationality. The Israelites adhered to the "levirate marriage" system. This meant that a deceased husband's relative would marry the childless widow in order for an heir to be born and the family line to continue. This man would be called the kinsmen redeemer. Boaz was not the next of kin but worked to assure Naomi and Ruth the family line would continue. Ultimately the next of kin decided to pass over Ruth leaving Boaz the opportunity to gladly take Ruth as his wife. This is more than a happy romance movie. I know this seems like a lot, but bear with me.

Read Ruth 4: 21-22. Draw a small family tree in the margin. Noting where Ruth falls into the line.

Now Read Jeremiah 23:5-6.

I'm in awe of how God changed this woman's life from being barren for ten or so years to becoming a mother — all the while being a part of the generational line of Jesus. What a story of redemption and grace! Ruth, Rahab and Tamar are all women who were brought into the family of God not because of their nationality but because of their faith. God's sovereign hand chose these women to be a part of Jesus' story of incarnation to show that His kingdom would one day be both Jews and Gentiles — on the ground of faith, justified by Christ's blood.

Journal:

1) How has God's sovereign hand guided you throughout this year?

2) How does Boaz as Ruth kinsmen redeemer mirror and foretell Jesus as our Kinsmen redeemer?

14
An Unlikely King

Scripture Reading: 1 Samuel 16:1-13 and 1 Samuel 17

Samuel walked into Jesse's home with the anticipation of immediately anointing a future king over Israel. Jesse's sons were lined up before him and appeared to all be of astounding stature. Just how a king should look. And yet, God continued to move Samuel past Jesse's other sons in search of David. David was a young shepherd boy; and though he was handsome, his small stature made one doubt his ability to ever be in a position of authority.

David was anointed king of Israel. Reread 1 Samuel 16:8.

The same can be said for David on the day he entered the battlefield against Goliath. Goliath, the Philistine giant, had caused the Israelites to cower before him. Yet, David boldly gathered his stones and sling shot, anticipating his imminent victory because of his trust in God.

David defeated the Philistine, Goliath.

These two situations were unlikely in the eyes of all those watching. How could David be the chosen one? But he was. David is referred to in scripture as "the man after God's own heart". And while David was not perfect or without sin, David truly grieved his sin and desired to honor God with his life.

Read 2 Samuel 7:1-17. What does God promise for the house of David?

Read Isaiah 11:10. Who is this root of Jesse who will rule all peoples?

God promised David a King who would rise up from his family line and would rule His kingdom forever; this King is Jesus! The two men are paralleled not only because of their genealogy line but because of their appearance on the stage of ruling their perspective kingdoms. David was touted as being incapable of being a king because of his youth, while those who were awaiting their Messiah were not expecting Jesus to die on the cross. Though the prophets consistently spoke to Jesus' death on the cross, the Messiah was assumed to be a valiant warrior or a mighty king who would sit on a physical throne — not an eternal throne.

God uses the unlikely. Redemption history continuously points to the fact that God uses men and women for His purposes despite their sin, despite their appearance, and despite their capabilities. Sweet friend, I would like you to know and trust that God uses you despite your sin, despite your insecurity of appearance, and despite your capabilities. God's plan for our salvation was set in place from the beginning of creation. David was a part of that plan. Jesus was the greatest part of that plan, and you, sweet friend, are a part of that plan.

Journal:

1) How is the story of David and Goliath a parallel of Christ defeating Satan?

2) Journal about the connection between the promises made to both Abraham and David.

3) How has God been using you for His purposes in unlikely circumstances lately?

15
The Prophets

Scripture Reading: See below.

I enjoy reading my Bible, that's a given; but, I really enjoy reading from the Prophets. They can be a bit confusing at times because I don't always know what they are talking about, but I do know they are almost always pleading with the Israelites for change. Turn back to God. Quit sinning. Cling to what they know to be true. Cling to what they've heard. Have faith in the One who has saved them. The prophets have various messages — all of which depend on Israel's history — pre, during, or post exile. And while much of their messages have a similar theme, we can't overlook the major prophecies spoken regarding the Savior to come!

I can't drive this point home enough! The promise was made WAY back in the garden to send one who would crush the serpent. Generations passed these promises down from one to another. And now, men are speaking direct words from God concerning the answer to this promise, and most of the people aren't listening. They continue to go about their own way.

Read the following passages. Journal about the significance of these prophetic messages as they relate and are connected to the birth of Christ. Each detail is so important. This will serve as our journaling for today.

Micah 5:1-5

Isaiah 60:3,6

Isaiah 7:14

Jeremiah 24:7

These are just a few examples of messianic prophecies from the Bible. Much was spoken about Jesus' life, death, and resurrection hundreds of years before His Incarnation. Though the Israelites heard their words, God sovereignly allowed the Babylonian takeover and the exile of His people to a foreign land. Their hearts did not cling to the hope the prophets spoke about.

Yet, He is ever faithful and kind. There was a remnant of people who heard the messages of Isaiah, Micah, and Jeremiah. And, they believed. We can be thankful for this remnant who continued to steadily walk in faith and honor the One True God. In their commitment to their God, they faithfully passed down the promises of God to the next generations.

Though I believe God is the one who saves, I also hold to scripture; we are commanded to tell others. The prophets used every moment to tell a stubborn nation of Christ's coming and their need to return to God. May we do so likewise and with a fervent heart — telling those we love the most and those we don't know at all that Jesus Christ is our Savior!

16
Silence

Scripture Reading: Daniel 7 and 8

"Long lay the world in sin and error pining."

Silence. I've nestled myself into a comfy spot to begin writing today. The candle is lit. The windows are open. There is a chill in the air, and there is not a drop of noise to distract me at the moment. I relish it.

Though this need not be a profound statement, silence is merely the absence of noise and sound. Of the 66 books found in the canon of Scripture that are neatly divided between both the Old Testament and New Testament, there rests a span of a mere 400 years between the ending of Malachi and the beginning of Matthew. These 400 years are often called the Silent Years and referred to theologically as the Intertestamental period, appropriately so. I wanted to highlight this time period during the Advent season particularly because it was during this span of 400 years that the Israelites did not hear a prophetic word spoken about the coming King. Today's scripture reading is Daniel's prophetic visions as to what would happen during this time period. To be sure Israel was taken over by several kingdoms and life continued on; and for historical purposes it should be noted at the close of this period of silence and at the arrival of Jesus to Earth, the Roman government was ruling over Jerusalem. However, despite all of these changes politically, socially and economically, the prophets ceased speaking.

Can you imagine what that must have been like? I'm sure the Israelites knew of the warnings the promises of God to save His people. They'd been hearing them all their life. They had heard of turning from sin and a king would come to reign. They knew *someone* would come and crush their enemies. But there was silence. There were no Isaiahs or Joels or Habakkuks screaming repentance from the rooftops. There wasn't a Jeremiah begging for the Israelites to return to the Lord. There was just silence. And though the Israelites did not heed their warnings when the prophets were speaking the words of the Lord, I imagine they felt a little lost without hearing the constant buzz of those warnings.

I liken it to this example, which is an example on a very small scale — For those of us who have to fall asleep to the hum of a fan it often becomes so present in our sleep routine that we forgot about it. We forget about it and go into automatic mode each night, until for some strange reason it stops its hum. In the middle of the night when the electricity goes out during a storm, we realize the importance of that hum in our nighttime routine. And maybe, just maybe, there were some men and women who had heard whispers of a Savior to come and were wondering just where He might be. Had His promises failed? Had they been forgotten?

Oh, no! They had not been forgotten. There was never a moment in time when God's people were not in His sight. (Can we just think about that for a minute?). In the fullness of time, the silence would break, and God would send His Son into the world to save the sinner. The thrill of hope! There was the voice of one crying out of His coming! The weary world rejoiced because the silence was broken!

We've already acknowledged the holiday season can be difficult for some people — add to that the time change and the day being shorter; the leaves falling on the ground; colder temperatures; and just the dead of winter — and we can just feel like crawling in a hole sometimes until Spring comes back. My husband doesn't call me his sunflower without good reason! It can easily feel as if God is distant when looking outside at a drab and dreary sin. It may even feel like He's being silent. For years, I equated the winter months with a distant heart from God. But friends, don't let that be the case. Know that even in the silence, He has you and hasn't forgotten you. There is One who has come that gives us life and His Spirit. There is One who has saved us, redeemed us and called us His own. There is One who is our King and Lord — He is our Messiah. He is the One the Israelites waited years for, but He is alive and reigning now. We don't have to wait any longer. We don't have to fear the silence. We can cry out to Him! We can call on His Name in the dead of silence.

Journal:

1) Has there been a time in your life where you have felt like God was being silent?

2) How can silence been seen as a good thing on our often hard days?

17
Joy to the World! The Lord is Come!

Third Candle of Advent: Joy

Scripture reading: Psalm 98

The Christmas season can be very busy. There are lists a mile long. Preparations to be made. Trees to be decorated. Gifts to be purchased; and not to mention, they need to be wrapped. With so much going on, it is easy for the little things to steal our joy.

Define happiness and joy. What is the difference between the two?

I like to think happiness is based more on the temporal. Activities and fun are great, but they can't and won't truly satisfy. I'm happy when I see my daughter scream in excitement. But these moments can't define our joy because they are fleeting and dependent upon circumstances. Joy is beyond the temporary and looks to the eternal. Our joy is defined by our contentment in Christ and what He has accomplished for us, regardless of our circumstances. For some, Christmas isn't the easiest of seasons. It serves as a reminder of loved ones lost or dreams that might possibly one day come true. Yet, these folks maintain a joy in their soul because of what Christ has done in their life. I'm sure you can think of a few people right now who fit this description. Joy is a constant state of contented quiet in Christ.

When I think of the Christmas season, I can't help but remember the many times our church group would go Christmas caroling in the neighborhood. It seemed "Joy to the World" was the staple Christmas carol to sing at every house. Hot chocolate and sweet treats were the prize when we returned from singing in the cold.

While our Advent devotion has focused on the incarnation of Christ, it wasn't until I began to study some of these treasured Christmas hymns that I learned "Joy to the World" really wasn't about Jesus' birth. The writer, Isaac Watts, meant it to be more of a hymn about Christ's second coming. And here we are. Are you as surprised as I am?

Watts wrote "Joy to the World" to paraphrase Psalm 98 and point to the New Testament promises of a coming Kingdom. Therefore, the hymn was primarily written with eternity in mind and not Christ's birth. Let earth receive her King! When Christ returns again, He will reign supreme. This is the joy of the Christian's soul. All that is. All that passes by. Our joy will be complete when He comes to take us home.

We can certainly allow our conditions and activities define our ideal Christmas. But let us not forget joy surpasses it all. Our joy is complete in Christ — what He has accomplished; what He is accomplishing; and what He will accomplish when He returns.

Joy to the World! The Lord is come! Let earth receive her King!![5]

Journal:

1) Do you find joy in your circumstances or in Christ?

2) Read Philippians 2:9-11, and explain the joy that will be for the Christian — as it relates to Watts' "Joy to the World."

---

[5] Isaac Watts, "Joy to the World," 1719.

18
Zechariah: How Shall I know?

Scripture Reading: Isaiah 40:3, Luke 1: 5-25

During the months that seemed to drag by of infertility, I often questioned God's reasoning and plan for my family's life. Would we have children? Would we adopt? Did He have greater plans for our lives involving serving college students, rather than having children of our own? On an afternoon walk, I began to list in my head the women from the Bible who were barren for quite some time. They flooded my mind as I realized there were more than just one, and I wasn't alone — Sarah, Rebekah, Ruth, Hannah, and Elizabeth. As I began to pray aloud on my walk (and I'm sure my neighbors thought I was crazy), I realized the perfect timing of the Father in gifting these women with children when He did. He does nothing by happenstance, and His ways are perfect. Each woman brought forth a child who was used mightily for the Kingdom. Though these women were unable to see the purposes of God through their tears and prayers, God had His intentions at the forefront of every action. Their births were not ill-timed but were perfectly on time. Today and tomorrow we will look at Zechariah, Elizabeth and John the Baptist.

It is not by chance but rather with great intent that Zechariah was chosen to enter the temple of the Lord (Luke 1:9). I try to imagine what Zechariah might have looked like: creases along his brow line from years of toil and pain; an unsteady hand taking incense into the temple; an unprepared shock and awe as an angel appeared to him at that hour. To be certain, his prayers for a child, an heir, had been uttered many times before, and today was the day the Lord would grant his request. It was during this time an angel of the Lord revealed God's plans for Zechariah's family. His wife, Elizabeth, would give birth to a son who would make ready the people for the Messiah's appearing; the child's name would be John. While I was reading today's passage, I was struck by the intimacy of the moment. God sent his messenger to appear to Zechariah at a time and place where no one else could be around to hear the news. This was a message specifically for Zechariah. Not only had their barrenness and shame been taken away, but this child, their son, would play a major role in telling others of the Christ.

How I love what the angel deemed the appropriate response for Zechariah to be: "And you will have joy and gladness…" (Luke 1:14). The tide had turned. Things were going to change. Baby cries that were prayed for would now fill the room. Yet in the immediate news, Zechariah responded quite differently. Rather than awe and cries of excitement, there was doubt. In Zechariah's moment of unbelief, he was silenced until the arrival of his son. I can't imagine all of the things he pondered in his heart and mind during those long nine months. He knew the task his son would be called to carry forth. What a great and mighty task!

I would like to assume that I would respond differently than Zechariah did; however, that's more than likely not the case. His "Really God?" (my paraphrase) is oftentimes how I approach a situation. We are, in fact, a lot alike. I wring my hands in angst wondering why or how something has happened. This plays itself out as little trust in God and more trust in myself — control issues. God calls us to respond in faith through a variety of circumstances. Yet in God's great grace, He does not change His course of action because of our response. He continues forward and calls forth our faith each time. This is a part of our sanctification; and like Zechariah we are able to continue becoming more and more like Christ through each situation. As we prepare our hearts this holiday season and "prepare room" for Him, may we seek to remove those things that would cause us to respond to His direction with anything less than joy and gladness. Praise Him!

<u>Journal</u>:

1) What is something you have been presenting before the Lord in prayer for quite some time? Do you feel like God has somehow forgotten you over time?

2) Can you identify with Zechariah's response to the angel's news of him having a son? How does this situation show you God's grace

to us when our faith falters? On whom does our righteousness depend?

19
Preparing the Way of the Lord

Scripture Reading: Isaiah 40:3, Luke 1: 24-25; Matthew 11:1-19

Yesterday we focused on Zechariah, but today I'd like for us to take a look at Elizabeth and John the Baptist. Though we only get a few verses about Elizabeth in the story of the nativity; we can ascertain her excitement and joy of being pregnant. I am humbled by the dedication of Elizabeth and Zechariah to come before their God time after time and ask for a child, despite their circumstances. They did not allow their age to be a hindrance in their commitment to pray to the Lord; they knew God was able.

It must be noted the excitement Elizabeth must have felt when finding out she was pregnant. Sure, there were no pregnancy tests, but I imagine it did not take her long to put two and two together. And because of the prayers that had been prayed exhaustively, her heart was likely filled with joy and gladness — and possibly some anxiousness, fear, and thrill. Like any other woman, she began to prepare for the arrival of her baby. Though I do not know what that would look like for the time, but women had been having babies for years. I'm sure there were tips to be shared. All of the preparation would ready her family for the arrival of a sweet child into their home.

Prophets had spoken of one who would come to prepare the people for the arrival of the Messiah, but no one knew who he would be. Generations of people waited on this man to appear. They not only waited for the Messiah, but they also waited for His messenger. And here in the middle of a season of barrenness for a not-so-young Elizabeth and in the middle of a time of silence from all the prophets, one was being sent who would *PREPARE* them for the Savior! Isn't that what Advent is all about? The preparation and anticipation? In God's grace, He would send John the Baptist as one who would walk the roads and proclaim the coming of the Lamb and need for repentance. This child Elizabeth had so diligently prayed for was coming at just the right time and with great purpose. It was time for the Savior to come to earth, and thus it was time for His messenger to appear.

We know John the Baptist's ministry and ultimately his death were not easy. While in prison, John questioned the authority of Jesus Christ when he sent messengers to Jesus to be assured He was the Christ. The circumstances John found himself in - a dark, dank prison - seemed to be hopeless, when his life's task had been centered around the giving of hope to a lost world through news of Jesus Christ. However, Jesus assured John of the ministry He was carrying forth.

The entirety of John the Baptist's life story from birth to death is a sobering account of one who was born for a mission, yet his life ended in suffering when he was beheaded. What we must understand by looking at his life is that God has purpose for our lives, but it doesn't mean we escape suffering and/or hard times. Christ has overcome this world, and His kingdom is beyond the scope of what we see on this earth.

John the Baptist was born with great purpose; lived with great intent; and died with a greater picture of his eternity in Christ's kingdom. As we meet the demands of this season, may we be reminded of the Lord's purposes in our own lives. He is the sovereign who has us in the palm of His hand; however, that does not mean we escape and live a utopic lifestyle. Because our world is filled with sin, we will experience pain, suffering and hardship until Christ returns. Also, there are many who are hurting and grieving; there are many who are overjoyed for a season where they don't understand the True hope. Yet, we do not have to turn a blind eye to those situations. We, like John the Baptist, have been tasked to share the news of the gospel - the salvation that comes only through Christ- without questioning or hesitation. We are called to go and tell the good news!

May we respond to the demands of this season with both joy and gladness!

<u>Journal</u>:

1) Have you prayed diligently and exhaustively for something in your life, like Zechariah and Elizabeth? Has the Lord answered? How are you encouraged in your waiting by Elizabeth's story?

2) How has the Lord used a time of hardship or suffering to point you to the greater message of the gospel?

20
Mary, Did You Know?

Scripture Reading: Luke 1: 26-56

Today, I want to begin by directing your attention to a beautiful painting titled, "Virgin Mary and Eve", by Sister Grace Remington from Sisters of the Mississippi Abbey in Iowa.[6] If you've never seen this image, I ask you to take a moment to find it by searching the Internet. Several years ago, this painting made an appearance on my social media news feed, and the visual was astounding. Mary is pictured, with a full term belly, comforting the mother of all living Eve. A snake has entangled Eve's legs, and yet Mary stands with her foot on top of the snake. Let us know take the theology incorrectly; I want to add that Mary is not the actual one who will crush the serpent. We know that Jesus is the one coming to do just that, as promised in Genesis 3:15. But what a powerful image!

When Gabriel came to visit Mary and announced Christ's birth, I can't imagine the thoughts swirling in her head. An average teenaged girl, with preparations to be married, had her world turned upside down in a matter of moments. And yet her response was beautiful: "let it be to me according to your word" (Luke 1:38).

Mary knew of the long awaited Savior. She had heard of His coming. She knew, I believe, of her own sin and the need for salvation. Mary knew the Messiah would come, and thus she responded in faith.

Like all women, I believe Mary still needed some time to process and seek the Lord's discernment. Ultimately she accepted God's plans for her life, even if they were unexpected in the moment. This young mother praised God for how He would use her to bring salvation to the world through the incarnation of Christ. Without birth, there

---

[6]Sister Grace Remington, "Virgin Mary and Eve," 2005, Crayon and pencil drawing.

could be no death and resurrection. Reread Luke 1:46-56, and answer the following questions. This will serve as our journaling for today.

How does Mary begin or open her song? This is also known as "The Magnificat." (v. 46,7)

What are Mary's reasons for praising God?

How do you interpret verse 53? What are the people of Israel hungry for?

What promise to Abraham is Mary referring to in verse 55?

I want to end today's advent devotion with the following excerpt from an article I read while studying Mary's response:

[This] isn't something we should only ponder at Christmas. It's a way of living every day. When traffic delays us, when people disappoint us, when pregnancy surprises us, when both hardships and blessings come, may we be women who accept God's will as best. There's no greater status in the kingdom of God than that of a servant (Matt. 23:11).[7]

Mary trusted in the hand of her God and and praised Him for it. Immanuel was coming!

May we do likewise — "… fall on your knees, oh hear the angels' voices…".

---

[7] Melissa Kruger, "Saying Yes to God's Unexpected Plan" www.thegospelcoalition.org December 20, 2016. Accessed October 15, 2019.

21
All is Calm. All is Bright.

Scripture Reading: Luke 2:1-7, Ephesians 1: 3-10

During the calm of the morning, I sat in the silence of our house with the tree lit and darkness still looming outside. I began to hum the tune of "Silent Night, Holy Night." Oh, how I wish churches spent more time singing the Christmas hymns every Sunday morning of Advent, but unfortunately we oftentimes get one or two songs a Sunday. These songs are rich with theology and meaning. The lyrics kept circulating through my mind as I sat there… "All is calm…".[8]

The night of Jesus' birth was more than likely anything but silent. Imagine the animals of the stable hee-hawing and crowing; the rustle of hay; and not to mention the innocent cries of a baby - the awaited Messiah. There's nothing silent about anything in this scene. However, the silence and calmness are of a different kind than what merely describes that awesome night.

"All is calm" is not a line we have to sing just to describe the night of Jesus' birth. That night ushered in a calmness for all those who seek Him, for those who have faith in Him. Calm was ushered in that night as Mary undoubtedly experienced the pains of birth. There had to be some tears or gasps of agony. And yet, Calm came in the form of a babe who would be our Savior. The prophets had spoken of His birth in Bethlehem. They had spoken of His coming in way we didn't expect. And here He had come on a night to be remembered. Our Savior was/is our eternal calm in this diminishing sin-filled world.

Paul wrote to the Ephesians the blessings they would receive in Christ - "redemption through his blood, the forgiveness of our trespasses" (Eph. 2:7). The atonement for our sins was made by Christ; this is the calm we have. No longer do we have the wrath of God. No longer do we give empty sacrifices. No longer do we

---

[8] Franz Xaver Gruber, "Slient Night", 1818.

compare and despair. No longer do we have to strive. We celebrate the birth of Jesus looking to His death on the cross for us. In Him, we find our all. He is our righteousness. He is our hope.

As I sat in the dark silence, I was reminded of this calm and hope that we have in Christ. With Him as our Lord, He has sovereign rule over our lives. The Christmas season isn't just about trees and pageants or gifts. It is about worshipping and bowing to our King. With our great confidence to bow before Him, we can calmly look into the future knowing that He has us in the palm of His hands - the apple of His eye. We do not fear what may come, but we know that He has it all planned and directs our course. We affirm that He holds us and all things together. And so, we look each day, not just Christmas day, in the face during the silence of the morning and say, "All is calm".

Yes, all is calm.. and because of Jesus... all is bright.

Journal:

1) What fears or troubles have robbed your of rest and calmness this Christmas season? Make sure to take some time today to purposefully rest — physically, mentally and spiritually in Him.

2) How should the calmness of Christmas prepare us for a new year?

22
The Shepherds and All the Haste

Scripture Reading: Luke 2: 8-21

Over the weekend, Jeremy and I attended our church's annual Christmas program. This is always a bright spot in the holiday season, as the church gathers together to worship King Jesus with a special program and Christmas hymns. it seems to me as if the Christmas hymns were written with such care and the choicest words to display the excitement, anticipation and joy of the coming king.

Always the cynic with a critical eye, I had prayed specifically upon entering the sanctuary that the Lord would show me something new of this treasured, yet familiar story. I watched as the choir sang each note with elegance and reverberated words to musical notes that clearly displayed the creativity and gifts of God. In the center was the manger scene with Joseph and Mary cuddling their newborn babe. As the choir sang, my thoughts drifted to our own anticipation of birth and the arrival of our sweet girl. The doors then opened from behind and four men from the church dressed in shepherds' costumes hastily made their way to the front of the sanctuary. No doubt to take their marked positions around the manger. *Why were they walking so fast? Maybe they should slow down just a tad bit? This could not have been rehearsed. Don't they know this is a drama?* My thoughts swirled with criticism as I sat in the chair watching a scene of greatness unfold before me. Thankfully our Father doesn't leave us to our criticism and removes the mud and grime from our eyes to see the beautiful.

They *should* be walking with haste. Luke even chronicles their journey after hearing the message of the angels: "And they went with haste and found Mary and Joseph…" (Gen. 2:16). Why had they walked so quickly? It was not because they hadn't properly practiced their scenes. It was because they were shepherds in a field who knew of the coming Messiah and had waited long enough that there was no other response to be had except for run. In that moment my entire perspective shifted. The shepherds approached the stage and bowed at the manger. They were walking fast/running to the One who would be their Savior. The silence had lasted long enough. The words promised and prophecies passed down were being fulfilled in that moment. Simply this, there was no other appropriate response.

Ouch! Yes, it hurt in that moment - to see the shepherds run and bow at the manger. When was the last time we allowed ourselves to leap with joy at the revelation of Christ in our lives. We take the miraculous interventions of our God and count them mundane. And here, our Savior is coming again, but we/I sit and become so close-minded, focusing only on what is right in front of me. The Messiah has already come in the form of a babe and died on the cross for the atonement of our sins, AND He will be coming again to take us with Him!

This isn't a mindset that we often subscribe to; everything going on around us takes our attention. We get caught up in the day to day, especially this time of year with the jam-packed calendars. But we, like the shepherds, should be carrying on our days with haste and hope of Jesus' return. We should be seeking to adore Him and embrace His place on the throne of our lives.

Though the shepherds walked to the stage that afternoon in a great hurry, they showed me the reality of what each of us should be doing with our lives. We should be making haste to see Him in our daily lives; to worship Him in our daily lives; and to bring honor to Him in our daily lives, so that we can bow before Him as they did.

Journal:

1) What are some of the activities of Christmas that have taken your attention — ones that you have quickly approached doing, rather than focusing on the true meaning of Christmas?

2) How can you create an environment of worship in your home, so that those living under your roof daily desire to see Him and His work — just as the shepherds did on their journey to the manger?

23
The Gift of the Magi

Scripture Reading: Matthew 2: 1-12

The pageantry of the wise men in church Christmas plays has always fascinated me. They are adorned in beautiful robes that are brightly colored and bejeweled. Sometimes, they are even seen wearing floppy, quirky hats. Has anyone else seen the three kings dressed the way I described? Maybe I'm exaggerating it a bit, but their presence in the Christmas nativity can't be mistaken. And yet, according to scripture, these men did not actually visit baby Jesus on the night of His birth. The wise men came to visit about two years after Jesus was born.

The Gospel of Matthew was written primarily to a Jewish audience, and yet it is the only of the four gospels that records the visit of the wise men. I mention this because we see at the very beginning of our reading today that these men were from the east, which was likely Babylon. Therefore, they were not Jews. It is assumed these men had heard of the Messiah from the Jews who were exiled in Babylon.[9]

The Magi were not a part of the remnant of Israel. They had heard of the Messiah to be born because the Jews were faithful to tell of the One who was to come. If you have been a Christian for any time, we read the Christmas story often. We know it like the back of her hand. And yet, I've missed this! The Magi *had heard of the Messiah, and they believed*!!! And because they had heard and because they had believed, they acted. They left their homeland in faith to go and worship the King of Kings!

Read Numbers 24:17. What did the wise men follow to Bethlehem?

The wise men followed the star to where Jesus was located, so that they could bring gifts to Him and worship. The time and effort this

---

[9] "Matthew 2:2", The ESV Study Bible (Wheaton, IL: Crossway, 2008) 1822.

took is remarkable, but they continued on because they knew and believed Jesus was the Savior of the world. I wish I could adequately express how much This part of the Christmas story has taken on new meaning for me! All too often, I see and experience reasons to worship and praise God in the every day, and yet I fail to stop and acknowledge. I fail to stop and worship. And here are three men who are gifted beyond worldly standards and have humbled themselves to worship King Jesus.

Westward leading, still proceeding. Guide us to thy perfect light![10]

As we close today, I want to highlight one other aspect regarding the wise men. These men, as previously noted, were not Jews. And yet, their faith has justified them. The wise men's visit signifies God's inclusion of Gentiles into His family. Believers are not by nationality or race or color of the skin but by faith. The Gospel of Matthew closes with Jesus giving the disciples (and us) the Great Commission. We are commanded to tell all nations about Him!

Journal:

1) Are you being faithful to tell others about Jesus this Christmas season?

2) How can you use your home as a way to invite others in and share the love of Christ? (Note: This can be done year round.)

---

[10] John Henry Hopkins, "Three Kings of Orient", 1857.

24
Love Came Down

Fourth Candle of Advent: Love

Scripture Reading: Romans 5:1-11; 1 John 4:9-10

The season of Advent is more than just the Incarnation. While this is the reason we celebrate Christmas, we would be remiss if we failed to mention that Christ's birth and coming to earth is the epitome of God's love for HIs people. Because of God's great love for us, He sent His Son to earth to redeem us — sinners before the Holy God, living a life apart from Him. We needed a Savior. We needed Christ. The Incarnation is thus God's manifestation of His love for us.

Our salvation would be impossible if God had not sent His Son, Jesus, to bear our sins and guilt on the cross. Christ's resurrection on the third day signified the final sacrifice had been made; the propitiation for our sins are covered by His blood.

I have provided the lyrics to Shane and Shane's "Born to Die" in their entirety.[11] This song was featured on their 2008 Christmas album. I can't imagine a more appropriate way to end our day. If you have the capability of finding this song on a streaming service, please take a listen. Otherwise, thoughtfully read through these lyrics. I've said it on previous days, but Christmas and Easter go hand in hand. God's love for us is so great, and yet we often forget that enormous fact! God loves us. He loves us so much that He gave His Son. Take a listen, or a glimpse of the words below.

---

[11] Shane & Shane, "Born To Die," Glory in the Highest: A Christmas Record, Inpop Records, 2008.

Born to Die
Shane & Shane

One, two, three
When the babe was born
In a manger on the hay
God saw a veil torn
He saw Good Friday
He was born to die
Gold laid before the Christ
Incense, His presence is sweet
Myrrh to signify
Victory over death's sting
He was born to die
It came in a dream
To Joseph late one night
That Herod sought the King
But could not take His life
He was born to die
He said, "You don't take my life
You won't take my life
You don't take my life
I lay it down"
We came here today
To celebrate His birth
But let us not forget
Why Jesus came to earth
He was born to die
He was born to die
He was born to
He was born to die.

Journal:

1) Do you ever have a difficult time understanding or grasping God's love for you?

2) Have you ever considered the Incarnation of Christ to be a manifestation of God's love?

3) How have the lyrics to Shane & Shane's "Born to Die" changed your perspective of Christmas?

A Thrill of Hope

25
Christmas Day

Scripture Reading: Luke 2: 1-20

The stockings are hung by the chimney with care. The Christmas lights twinkle on the tree against the black sky of night. The toys have been unwrapped. The plates of delicious food and sweet treats have all been tossed aside. The excitement of all that has built up to Christmas Day has come to an end.

The cattle are mooing (as we teach our one year old), and the horses are neighing. The sheep are roaming around the stable. Their hooves scraping the cold, hard ground. The cries of a newborn babe pierce the night sky. And yet, the true excitement is just beginning.

Christmas is such a fast season. It comes and goes in the blink of an eye. We allow it to grow to a zenith and then dissipate, moving on to the next thing without truly remembering what we just celebrated. But that's not what God meant for us. The incarnation of Jesus was just the beginning. It was just the beginning of a plan that was set into motion many years ago in the garden with Adam and Eve. God provided and planned a way for His people to join Him again. Christ is the reason we celebrate this day and every day.

He — Jesus — is our thrill of hope. The world rejoices because He is the One who can take our burdens and give us rest. He is the One who heals the brokenhearted. He is the one who takes away our guilt and shame. He is the One. He is our Hope.

This Christmas we don't have to let it end when the sun goes down. Our hope in Christ lasts beyond just one day. If anything I hope this advent devotion has helped you see God's restorative work in the lives of many men and women. His hand is woven in their stories and our own. When we come to see how He works in our lives, we are able to fully, completely worship Him.

Let your worship continue. Let your praise continue. Let your sharing the love of Christ with family and friends continue. It is not limited to one season. No, it is for now and tomorrow and next month.

A thrill of hope. The weary world rejoices. Let all within us praise His holy Name!

PREPARING YOUR HOME: INTENTIONAL GATHERINGS

The warmness of the holiday season is the perfect time to invite friends and family into your home. If this isn't a regular occurrence for your family, make the Christmas season a starting point for opening your home to others all year long. I have provided a few ideas to get you thinking in the right direction for intentional gatherings. Intentional doesn't necessarily mean the gospel has to be presented every time someone walks into your home for a meal. But it does provide an opportunity to get to know those around you and exhibit Christ to them by serving them in your home.

Christmas With a Cause Party
This always worked well for a girl's night. Several weeks before the party date, I would inform my guests our "cause" for the year. One year we made bags for elderly at the nursing home with stationery, lotions, etc. While another year, we made bags for the women who entered the doors of a local pregnancy center. We included cozy socks, lotions, candles etc. You can also adopt a family through your church. Each guest brought items they wanted to donate to the bags and an appetizer to share. It's not a party without food! We assembled the bags together; prayed over the bags; and then enjoyed time chatting and eating, of course!

Mexican Fiesta Dinner
I like to serve a meal of delicious Mexican food at some point during the holiday season. It often happens on January 6th for my family, which is known as Epiphany or Coming of the Wise Men Day. While on a mission trip in Mexico during Epiphany, we were able to celebrate with the church plant. They had a huge Mexican feast and exchanged gifts. Serving Mexican during the holiday season can always be a conversation starter. Explain to your guests how other countries celebrate Christmas and the importance of Epiphany.

Christmas Caroling

Christmas caroling is a lost art. I loved going door to door and singing for people in our neighborhood. Revive this lost art. Set a date, and invite your friends over to sing to the neighbors in your neighborhood. It may be helpful to type of a song list or paper hymnal for your guests. Don't forget to include classic Christmas hymns such as "Joy to the World." Invite your guests back to your house after singing for a few simple snacks and hot cider or hot chocolate! Children can easily participate in this as well.

PREPARING YOUR HOME: RECIPES

While it is of the utmost importance to prepare our hearts for the celebration of Christ's birth on Christmas day, our homes should be prepared as well. This doesn't mean our homes need to be decorated with ten Christmas trees or presents with matching wrapping paper. But it does mean our homes should be prepared to welcome others in during this holiday season. Whether a guest is staying overnight; coming over for an evening meal; or a quick cup of coffee, our homes should be a place of rest from the weariness of the world. Our homes are a safe haven, and the Christmas season is no better time than to invite others in and share a meal with them. The warmth of your home and inviting others in provides a platform for sharing the true meaning of the season with others. We don't have to be hurried or fretful over the meal. It just has to be simple and tasty. The worst of cooks can still invite others in. Below are a few recipes that remind me and the special people in my life of the Christmas season. Don't forget to add a festive napkin to your table. It makes any occasion extra special! (It can absolutely be a paper napkin!)

Appetizers and Beverage Recipes

Ham Poppy Seed Party Sandwiches

Ingredients:
1 12-count package of sweet rolls, sliced in half
1 package cooked deli ham, thinly sliced
1 package Swiss cheese
1 tablespoon poppy seeds
Yellow Mustard, or your preference
Butter, spreadable

Directions:
1. Preheat oven to 350 degrees. Line a 9x13 pan with aluminum foil, and spray with cooking spray.

2. Using a serrated knife, slice the rolls in half. These should be sliced so the "tops" and "bottoms" are separated. Place bread halves on preparation table with "inside" sides of the bread facing up.
3. Spread butter evenly on both "inside" parts of the sweet rolls. Spread mustard on bottom piece of bread.
4. Evenly layer cooked ham and swiss cheese. Optional: create two layers of ham and swiss inside sandwich for the meat-lovers at your party.
5. Sprinkle poppy seeds on top, buttered half of bread, and assemble bread back in place to create one large sandwich.
6. Bake covered for about 20 minutes, or until cheese has melted.
7. Uncover and cook for another 3 minutes.
8. Slice into individual sliders, and serve immediately.

Submitted by Teresa Gandy - Note: My mom (Erin, here) makes these every Christmas Eve. We always had heavy appetizers at my Mema's house on Christmas Eve. I loved these. But I especially liked eating the leftovers on Christmas morning while we opened presents, since we didn't do a big breakfast.

Christmas Meatballs

Ingredients:
1 lb. ground beef
1/2 cup onion, chopped
1/2 cup of water
1/2 cup of bread crumbs
1 1/2 teaspoon salt
1/2 teaspoon nutmeg
flour
butter

Gravy Ingredients:
1 1/4 cup water
1 cup milk
1/2 teaspoon salt
1/2 teaspoon nutmeg
flour

Directions:
1. Combine ingredients, and shape into meatball form.
2. Dredge each one in flour.
3. Melt 2 tablespoons of butter in a large frying pan.
4. Add meatballs, and brown slowly for about 20 minutes.
5. Remove meatballs from pan.
6. Mix together gravy ingredients in frying pan.
7. Pour gravy over meatballs.

Submitted by Amanda O'Bryan, Erin's bestie

Quick Apple Cider

Ingredients:
1 bottle of apple juice
1 bag of cinnamon candies

Directions:
1. Pour desired amount of apple juice into a medium sized pot.
2. Warm over medium heat.
3. Add cinnamon candies to apple juice, occasionally stirring so candies do not stick to the bottom.
4. Serve in festive mugs once candies have melted completely.

Submitted by Erin Stache

Breakfast Recipes

Breakfast on Christmas morning is always a special time. Whatever the size of your family, everyone can gather around the table for a warm, comfy, belly-filling breakfast before the day's celebrations begin.

Christmas Breakfast Casserole

Ingredients:

1 pound ground pork sausage
1 teaspoon mustard powder
1/2 teaspoon salt
4 eggs, beaten
2 cups milk
6 slices of white bread, toasted and cut into cubes
8 ounces of mild cheddar cheese, shredded

Directions:
1. Crumble sausage into medium skillet. Cook over medium heat until evenly brown. Drain.
2. In a medium bowl, mix together mustard powder, salt, eggs, and milk. Add the sausage, bread cubes, and cheese. Stir to coat evenly. Pour into a greased 9x13 inch baking dish. Cover, and chill in the refrigerator for 8 hours, or overnight.
3. Preheat oven to 350 degrees.
4. Cover, and bake 45 to 60 minutes. Uncover, and reduce heat to 325 degrees. Bake for an additional 30 minutes or until set.

Submitted by Amanda O'Bryan and Darlene McLain, Erin's bestie and her mom

Baked French Toast Casserole with Maple Syrup

Ingredients:
1 loaf French bread (13 to 16 ounces)
8 large eggs
2 cups half-and-half
1 cup milk
2 tablespoons granulated sugar
1 teaspoon vanilla extract
1/4 teaspoon ground cinnamon
1/4 teaspoon ground nutmeg
Dash salt
Praline Topping, recipe follows
Maple syrup

Directions:

1. Slice French bread into 20 slices, 1-inch each. (Use any extra bread for garlic toast or bread crumbs). Arrange slices in a generously buttered 9 by 13-inch flat baking dish in 2 rows, overlapping the slices. In a large bowl, combine the eggs, half-and-half, milk, sugar, vanilla, cinnamon, nutmeg and salt and beat with a rotary beater or whisk until blended but not too bubbly. Pour mixture over the bread slices, making sure all are covered evenly with the milk-egg mixture. Spoon some of the mixture in between the slices. Cover with foil and refrigerate overnight.
2. The next day, preheat oven to 350 degrees F.
3. Spread Praline Topping evenly over the bread and bake for 40 minutes, until puffed and lightly golden. Serve with maple syrup.

Praline Topping Instructions:
   1/2 pound (2 sticks) butter
   1 cup packed light brown sugar
   1 cup chopped pecans
   2 tablespoons light corn syrup
   1/2 teaspoon ground cinnamon
   1/2 teaspoon ground nutmeg

Combine all ingredients in a medium bowl and blend well. Makes enough for Baked French Toast Casserole.

Submitted by Amanda O'Bryan

Side Dish Recipes

Some people will argue with me about this one, but I think a good side dish "makes" a meal. More than likely, people are going to remember what else you had on the table besides the anchor entree item. Make these easy, special dishes for your next occasion!

Sweet Potato Casserole

Ingredients:
3 cups sweet potatoes, mashed
1 cup sugar

1/2 teaspoon salt
2 eggs, beaten
1/2 stick margarine, melted
1/2 cup milk
1 teaspoon vanilla flavoring

Nut topping:
1 cup brown sugar
1/3 cup plain flour
1/2 stick margarine, melted
1/2 cup pecans, chopped

Directions:
1. Preheat oven to 350 degrees.
2. Combine ingredients for casserole in a medium sized bowl. Mix ingredients for nut topping in a separate bowl.
3. Spoon casserole mixture into prepared 9x13 dish. Sprinkle nut topping on top.
4. Bake for 35 minutes.

Submitted by Eleanor Lawhon, Erin's Mema

Apple Cobbler

Ingredients:
2 1/2 cups sliced apples
1 cup all purpose flour
1 cup white sugar
1/2 teaspoon cinnamon
1/2 cup water
1 stick of margarine, cut into square chunks

Directions:
1. Place a sliced apples into bottom of prepared casserole dish.
2. Add 1/4 cup to 1/2 cup water to apples in casserole dish.
3. In a medium bowl, mix together dry ingredients, and sprinkle over apples.
4. Place chunks of margarine on top of dry mixture.

5. Bake at 350 degrees for 45-50 minutes, until golden brown on top.

   Submitted by Cindy Weaver, Erin's Aunt

Green Bean Casserole

Ingredients:
1 can French style green beans, drained
1 can cream of mushroom soup
5-6 pieces of cooked bacon, torn into pieces
French fried onions

Directions:
1. Mix all ingredients together in a medium sized bowl.
2. Bake at 350 degrees for about 25 minutes.
3. Make sure onion straws do not burn.

   Submitted by Priscilla Stache, Erin's mother-in-law. Note: This recipe takes the green bean casserole to the next level with all the bacon. It's a holiday favorite for me and Jeremy.

Mexican Street Corn Casserole

Ingredients:
32 oz. Frozen corn, thawed
1/2 cup mayo
1/2 cup sour cream
1.5 teaspoons chili powder
1/2 teaspoon garlic powder
1/2 teaspoon salt
5 oz Queso fresco or Monterey Jack cheese, shredded
cilantro, optional

Directions:
1. Preheat oven to 350 degrees.
2. Mix all ingredients until combined.

3. Bake 30-40 minutes until bubbly.
4. Top with queso fresco and cilantro.

Submitted by Erin Stache

Dessert Recipes

Christmas desserts are special treats. We wait all year long to have those certain desserts. Here are a few recipes that have me and others thinking fondly of the Christmas season.

Peppermint Brownie Trifle

Ingredients:
1 Brownie mix, prepared and baked per instructions
1 large box of chocolate instant pudding, prepared per instructions
1 large container of whipped topping
1 packaged of peppermint or mint baking bits

Directions
1. Once all components have been prepared and sufficiently cooled, begin assembling the trifle.
2. Cut brownies into bite size pieces, and place at the bottom of the trifle dish.
3. Next layer with chocolate pudding and cool whip. Sprinkle peppermint pieces on top of the whipped topping.
4. Continue layering brownie, pudding, whipped topping, peppermint pieces until trifle is complete.
5. End with cool whip and peppermint pieces.

Submitted by Erin Stache

Easy Festive Ice-cream Pie

Ingredients:
1 container of vanilla ice-cream, softened

1 package of mint chocolate sandwich cookies, crushed into smaller pieces where icing color is still apparent
1 package of red-filled chocolate sandwich cookies, crushed into smaller pieces where icing color is still apparent
1 or 2 chocolate graham cracker pie crusts

Directions:
1. In a medium sized bowl, mix softened vanilla ice-cream and festive sandwich cookies.
2. Scoop mixture into graham cracker pie crusts.
3. Refreeze until ready to serve.

Submitted by Erin Stache

Chocolate Crinkles

Ingredients:
2 cups and 2 tablespoons flour
2 teaspoons baking powder
1/4 teaspoons salt
1/2 cup butter (room temp)
3 eggs
1 teaspoon vanilla
1/2 bottle mint
4 squares (1 oz each) unsweetened chocolate, melted
confectioners' sugar

Directions:
1. Mix together dry ingredients.
2. Beat butter and sugar together using an electric mixer.
3. Add eggs, and beat until pale yellow.
4. Add vanilla, mint, and chocolate.
5. Gradually add dry ingredients to mixing bowl.
6. Refrigerate for 15-20 minutes.
7. Shape dough into 1/4 inch balls, and roll in confectioners' sugar.
8. Bake at 350 degrees for 12 minutes.

Submitted by Amanda O'Bryan - Note: These cookies always remind me of my former roommate Jen's Cookie Days. Christmas Cookie Day was a family tradition she shared with me and our friends when we lived together.

Quick Snacks and Treat Recipes

The Christmas season is always an exciting time of the year where we have those "special"" treats. These are just a few that I enjoy making and eating! Share these easy treats and a "Merry Christmas" with some friendly folks in your life — coworkers, the postman, your neighbors, etc.

Divinity Candy

Ingredients:
3 cups sugar
1/2 cup light corn syrup
1/2 cup cold water
2 egg whites, beaten until stiff
1 teaspoon vanilla
chopped pecans

Directions:
1. Boil sugar, syrup, and water.
2. While this is beginning to boil, beat egg whites and set aside.
3. Boil mixture until it forms a thread when you drop it from the spoon while stirring.
4. Turn mixer on low while pouring mixture over egg whites.
5. Add vanilla and nuts.
6. Spoon onto wax paper in dollops.

Submitted by Eleanor Lawhon

Ranch Trash Mix

Ingredients:
8 cups crispy corn cereal
3 cups of small pretzels
3 cups of bite size cheddar cheese crackers
5 cups of plain oyster crackers
1 cup vegetable oil
1 small envelope of Ranch salad dressing mix

Directions:
1. Preheat oven to 250 degrees.
2. Mix all together.
3. Pour vegetable oil over mixture over mix, and coat.
4. Sprinkle dressing packet over mix, and stir. Optional: toss all together inside a grocery bag or large Ziploc.
5. Cook on a sheet pan for 15-20 minutes.

Submitted by Eleanor Lawhon and Teresa Gandy

Chocolate Clusters

Ingredients:
Melting chocolate, white or milk chocolate
Cluster items - peanuts, pecans, marshmallows, pretzel pieces, etc.
Wax paper

Directions:
1. Pour all cluster items in to a medium sized bowl, and stir.
2. Prepare melting chocolate per package instructions. Most come in a tray and require stirring every so often.
3. Pour melted chocolate over mixture in bowl, and quickly stir.
4. Drop clusters on wax paper, and allow to set.

Submitted by Erin Stache

Tar Heel Pie

Ingredients:

1 cup chocolate chips
1 stick butter, melted
1 cup chopped pecans
1 teaspoon vanilla
1/2 cup plain flour
1/2 cup white sugar
1/2 cup brown sugar
2 eggs, beaten

Directions:
1. Pour warm butter over chocolate chips, and stir.
2. Blend all remaining ingredients and stir into chocolate chip mixture.
3. Pour into unbaked pie shell.
4. Bake at 350 degrees for 30 to 40 minutes.

Submitted by Mrs. Cindy Bush, Erin's Wake Forest "mother". Note: Mrs. Bush makes these pies to give to her neighbors and friends.

A Thrill of Hope

Made in the USA
Coppell, TX
02 November 2019